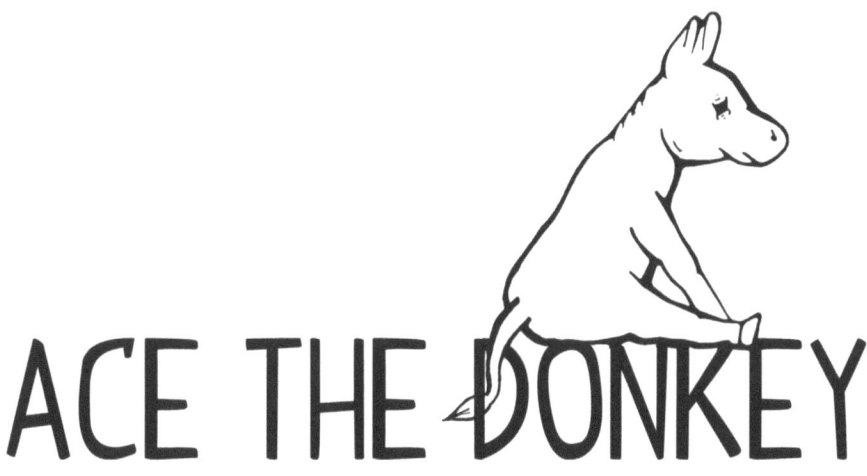

ACE THE DONKEY
BOOK OF ILLUSTRATED A** WORDS

WRITTEN AND ILLUSTRATED
BY MICHAEL RAGSDALE

JOHN 12:14,15

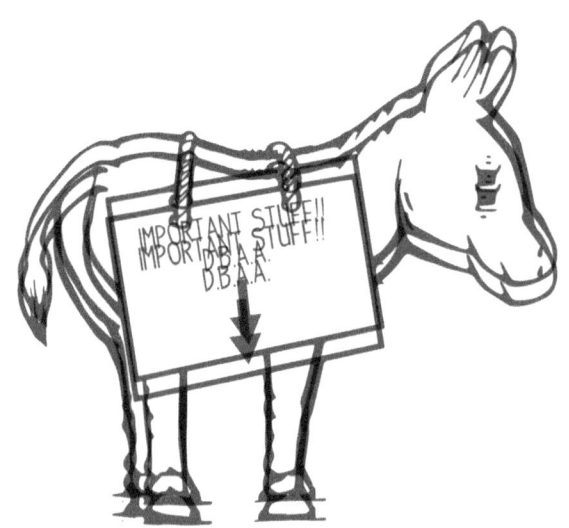

Copyright © 2020 by Michael Ragsdale

All rights reserved. No part of this book may be reproduced or used in any manner without written permission of the copyright owner except for the use of quotations in a book review. For more information, address: michaelragsdaleart@gmail.com

FIRST EDITION

ISBN 978-1-716-93961-7 (paperback)

www.ragzillo.com

@ragzillo

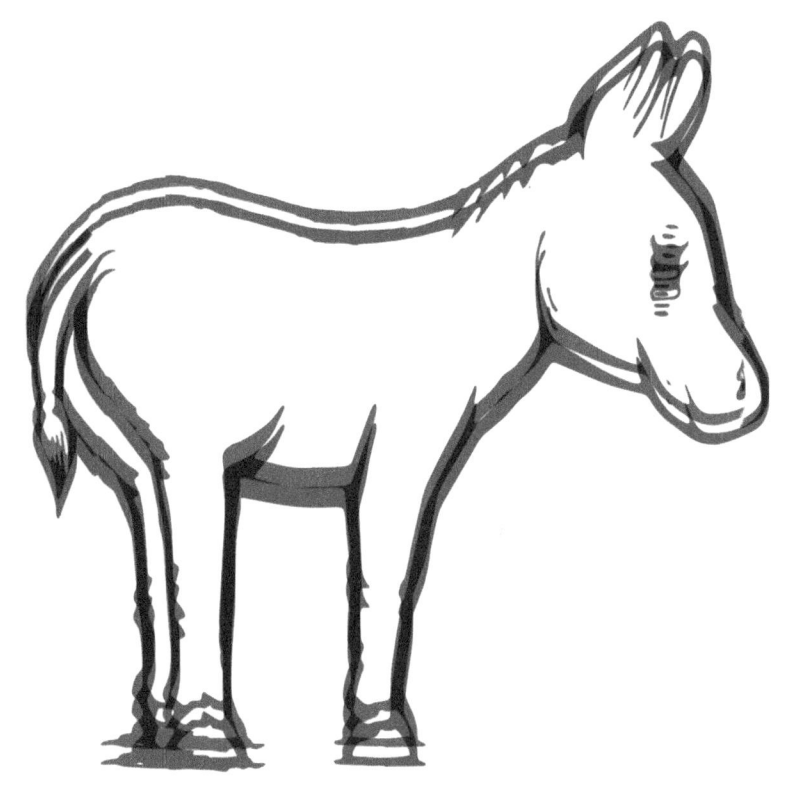

MEET ACE.
ACE, AS YOU CAN SEE, IS A DONKEY (SOME MAY CALL HIM, AN ASS).
HE WOULD LIKE TO INVITE YOU TO GUESS THE "ASS" WORD OR
PHRASE IN EACH OF HIS ANTICS THROUGHOUT THIS BOOK.

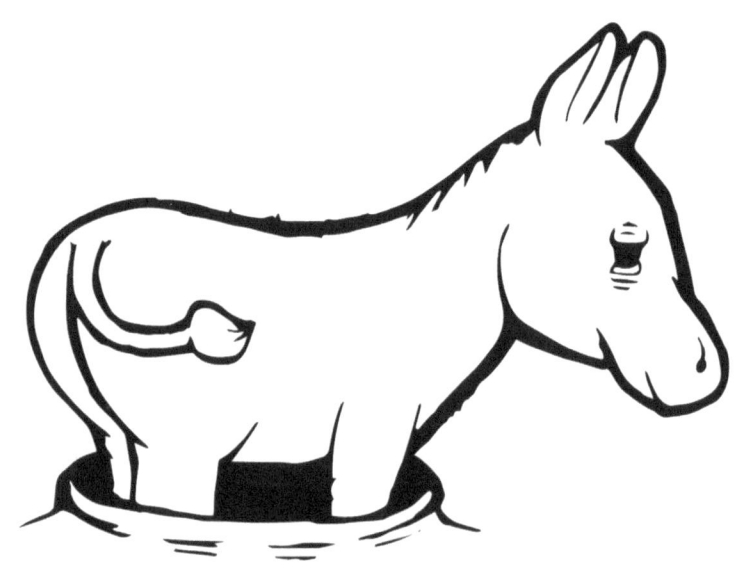

ACE IS BEING A JERK ABOUT FALLING INTO THIS HOLE.

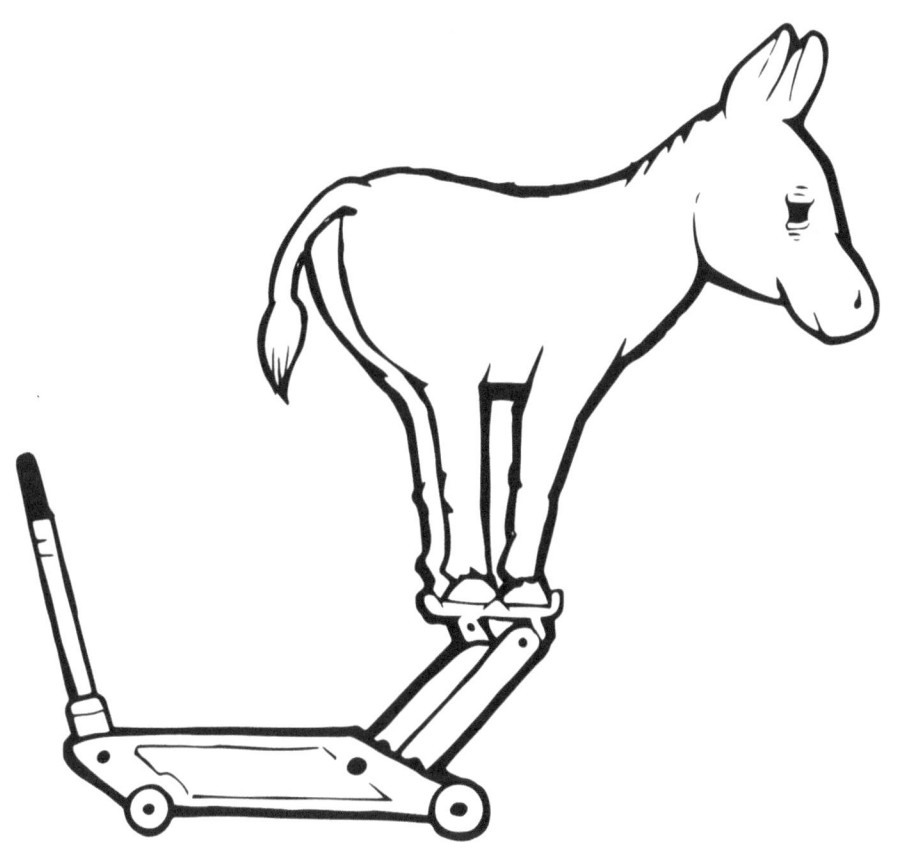

ACE IS BEING STUPID AND PLAYING WITH THINGS HE SHOULDN'T.

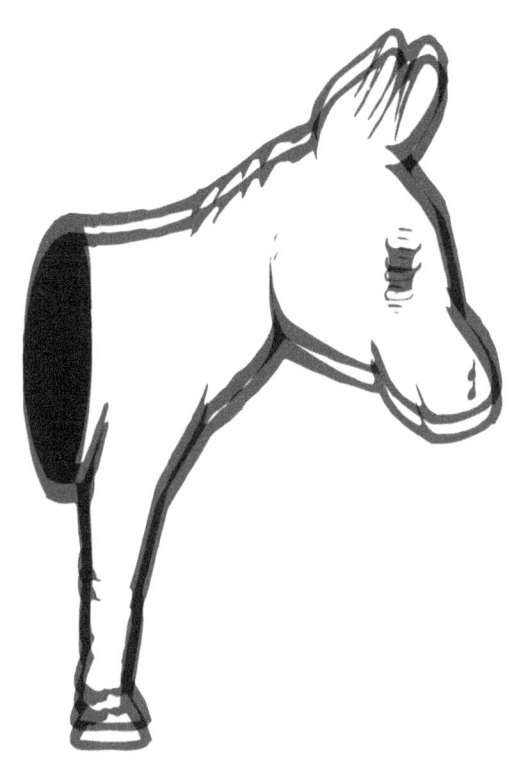

HALF AN ACE WILL ONLY GET HALF THE RESULTS.

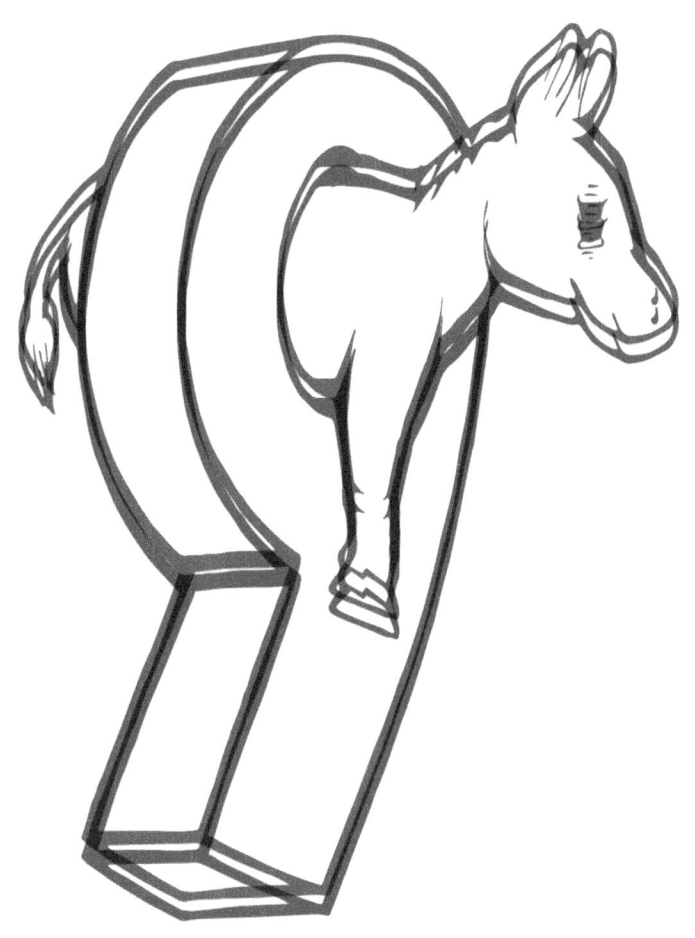

WELL:::THIS IS ABSURD:

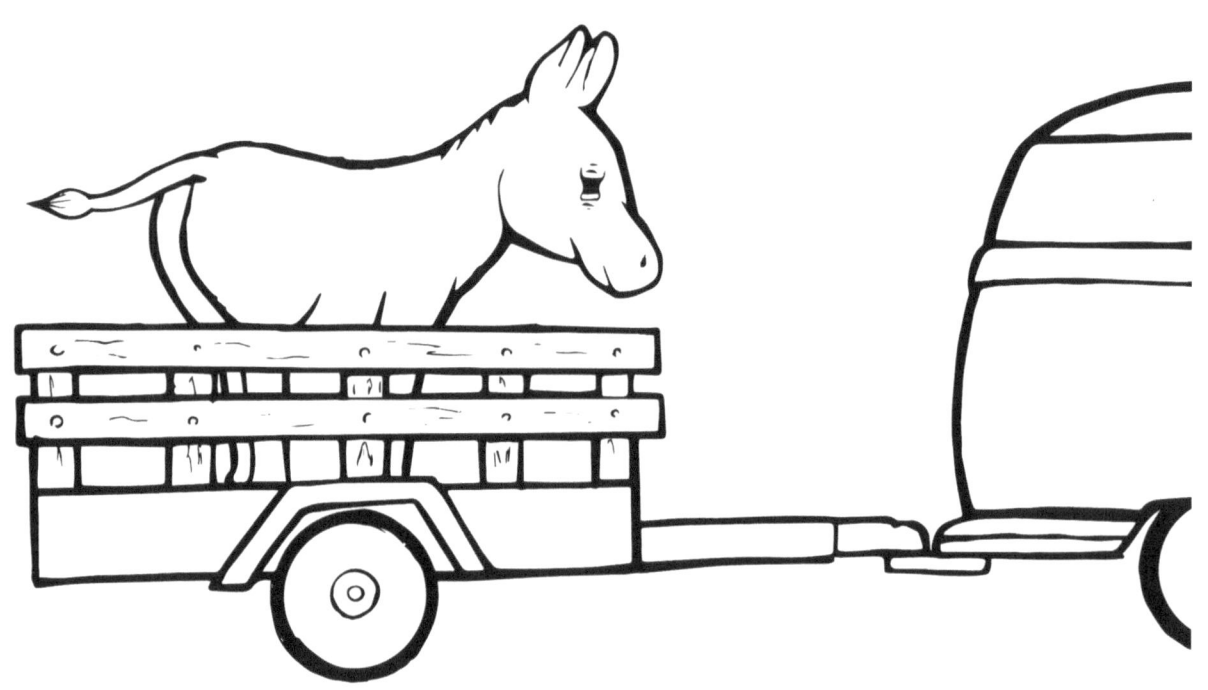

WHERE IS ACE GOING IN SUCH A HURRY?

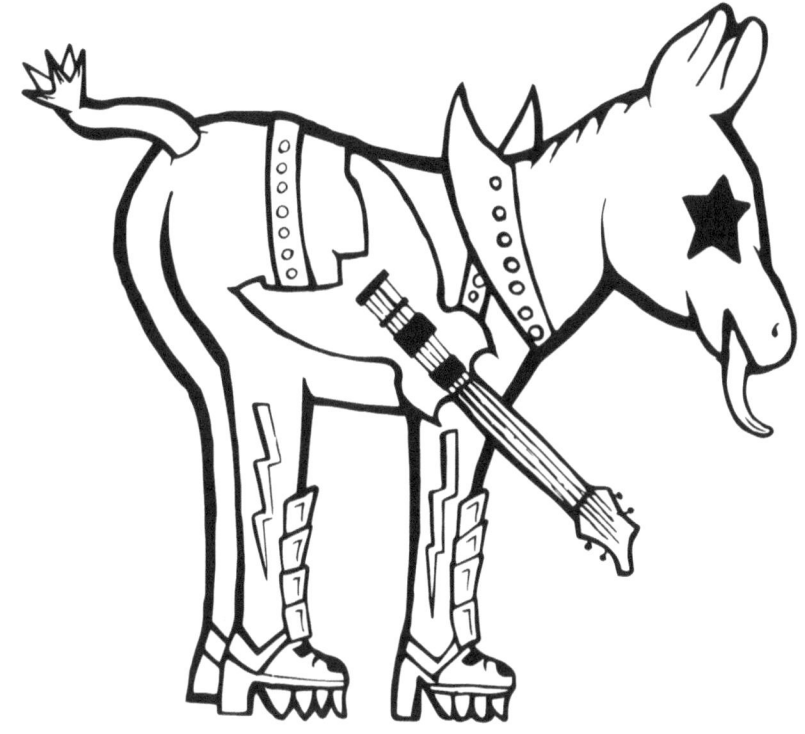

ACE IS STARTING A TRIBUTE BAND.

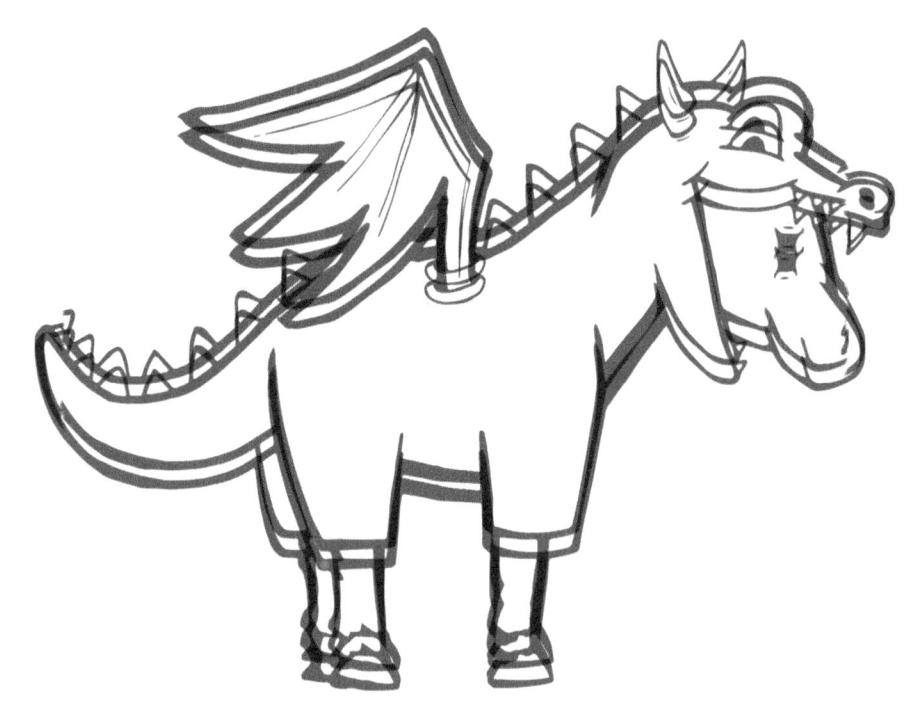

ACE IS FEELING VERY SLUGGISH TODAY:

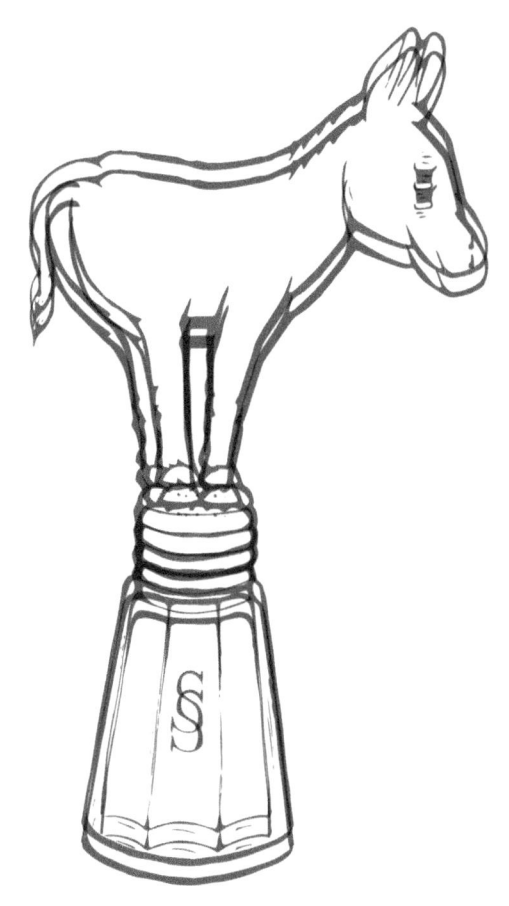

ACE NEEDS TO GET OFF THAT SHAKER AND SHOW IT SOME RESPECT.

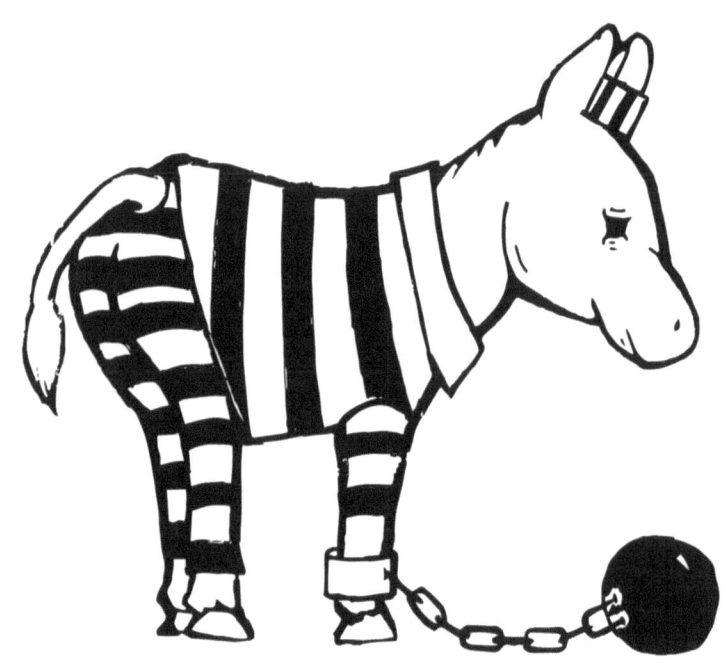

ACE GOT HIMSELF INTO SOME BIG TROUBLE.

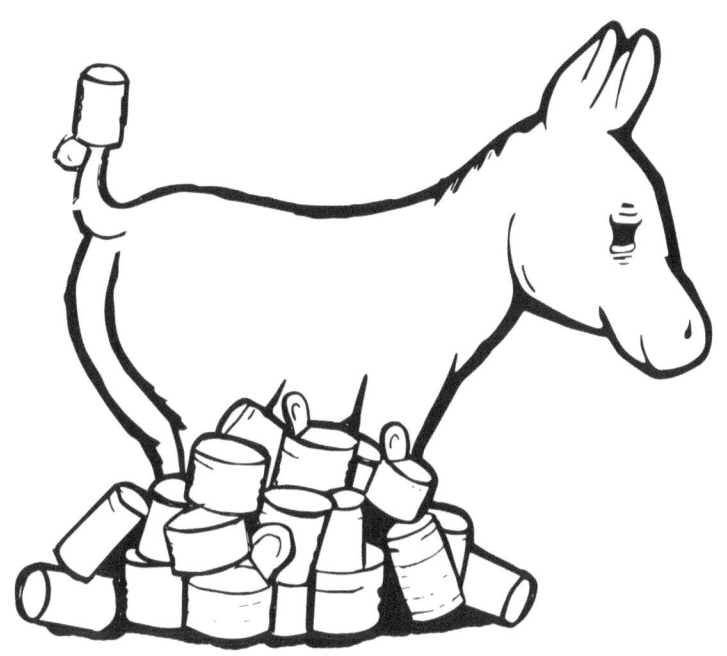

ACE IS IN A STRANGE STATE OF MIND.

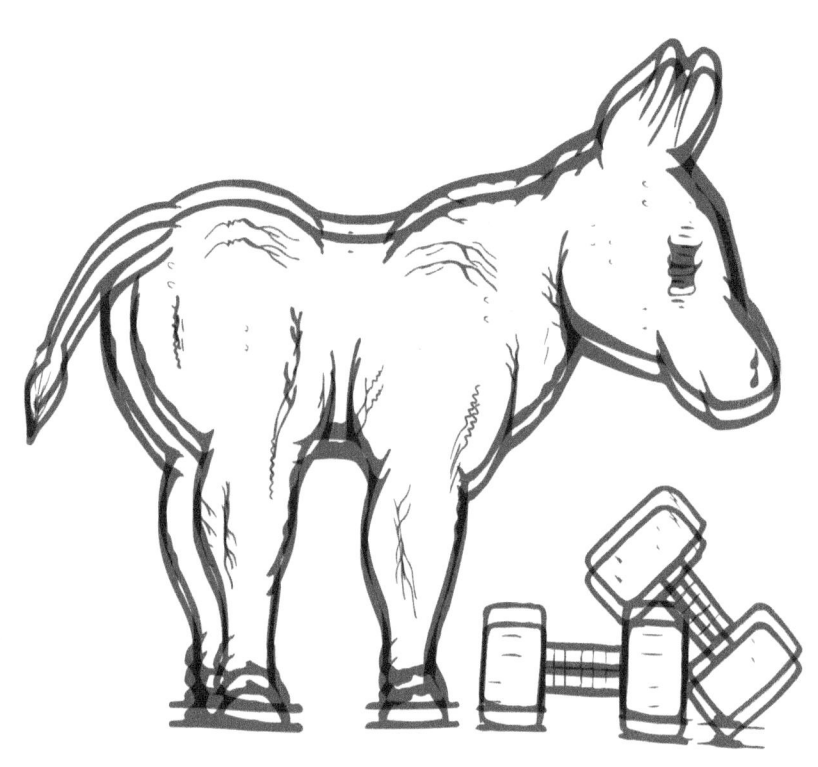

ACE IS SWOLE...ILLEGALLY.

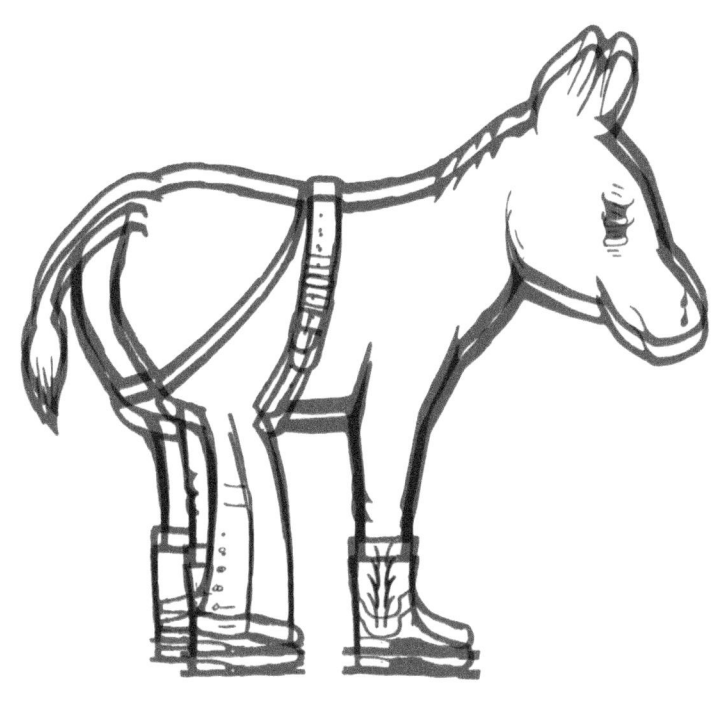

ACE IS PISSED OFF:

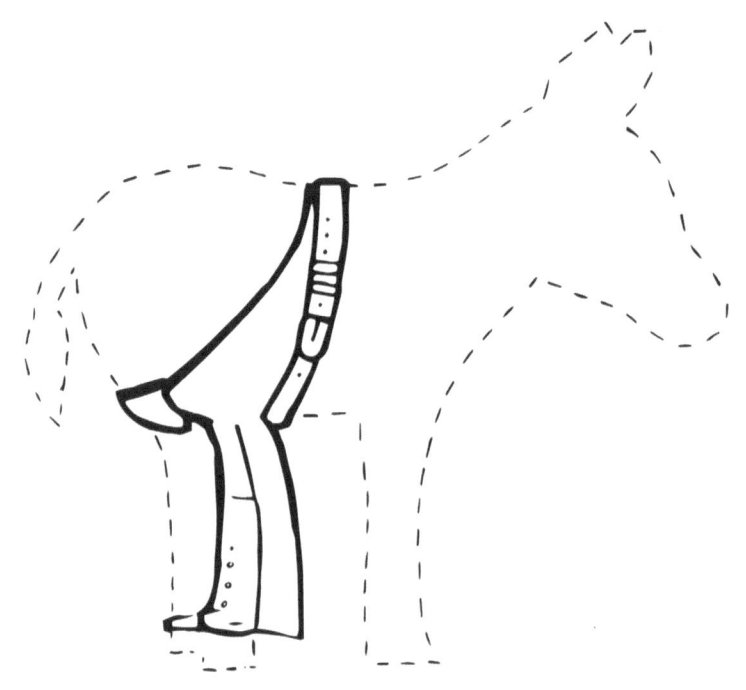

WHERE IS ACE?

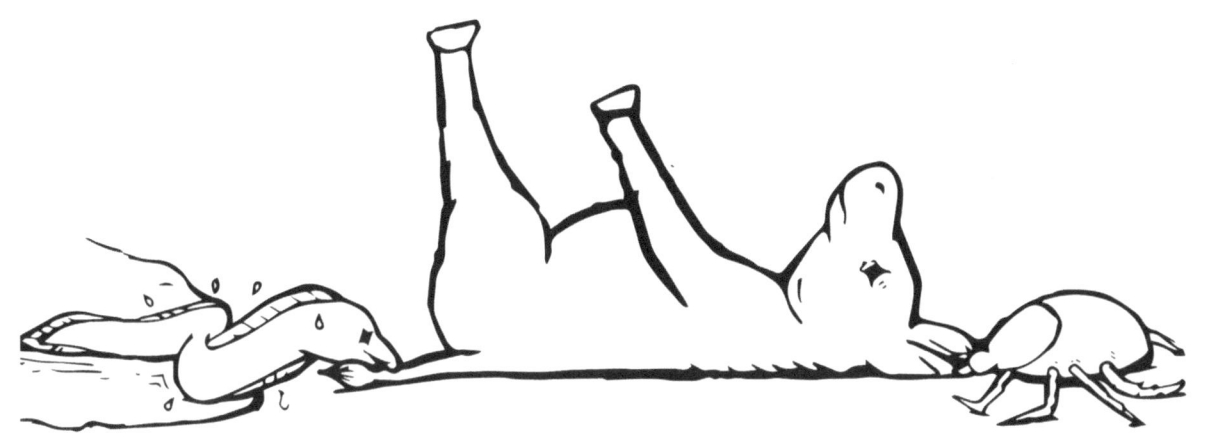

ACE IS GETTING STRETCHED OUT.

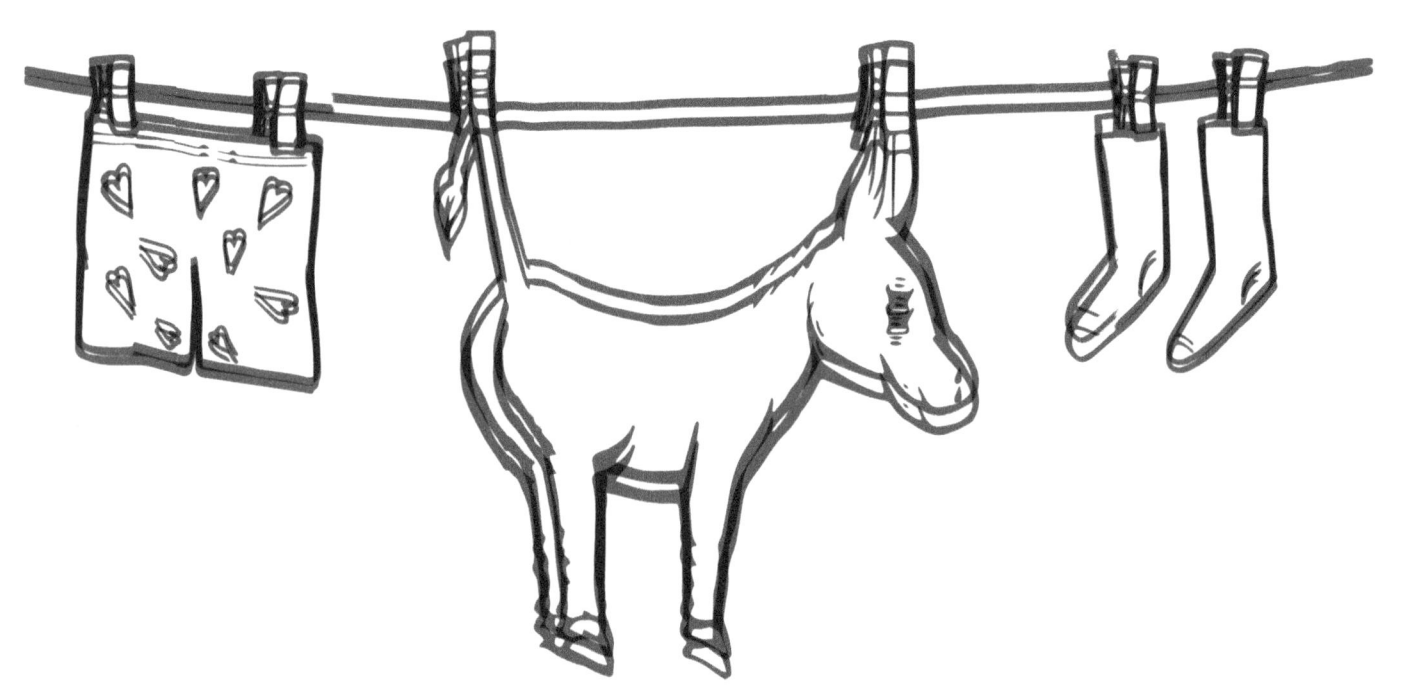

ACE WAS DITCHED AND LEFT TO HIMSELF.

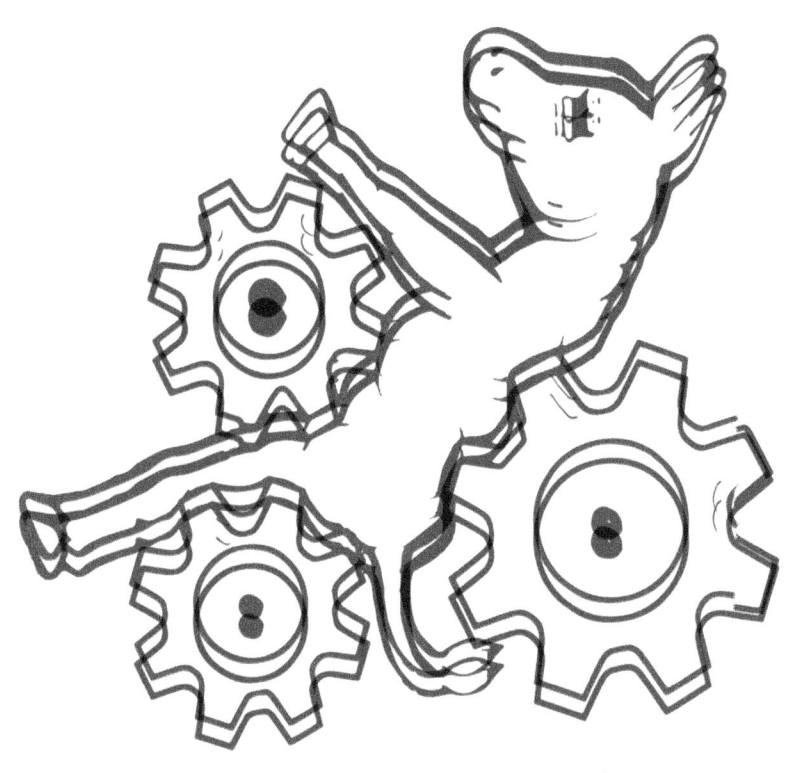

ACE BETTER GET HIS ACT TOGETHER IF HE WANTS TO GET OUT OF THIS MESS.

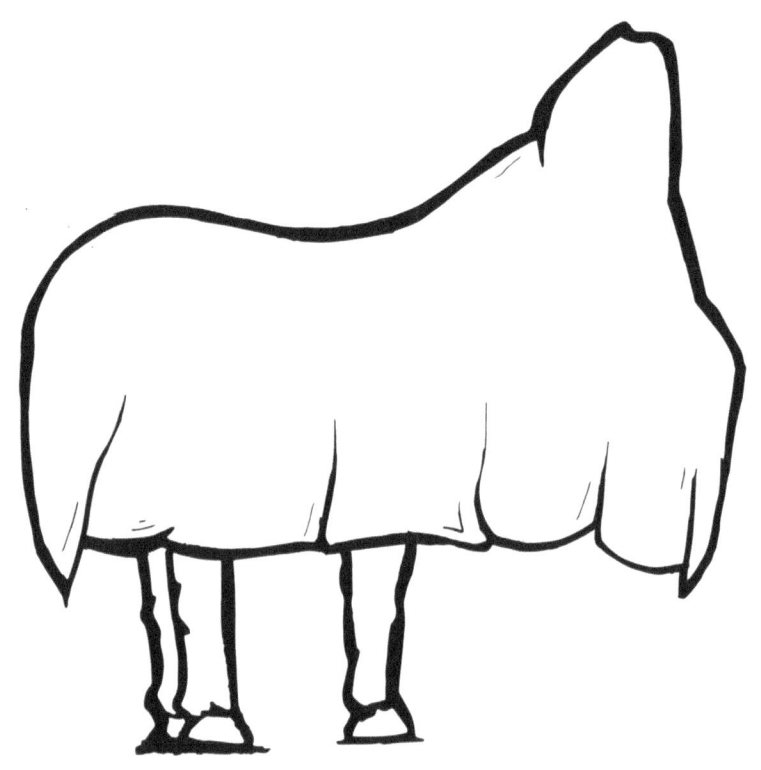

ACE WILL BE PROTECTED UNDER THIS SHEET.

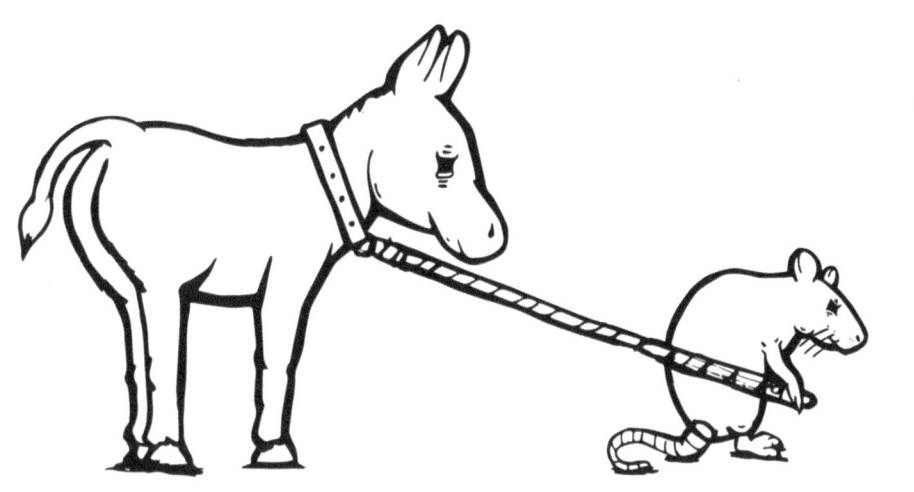

THIS RAT DOESN'T CARE WHAT PEOPLE THINK OF HIS PET ACE.

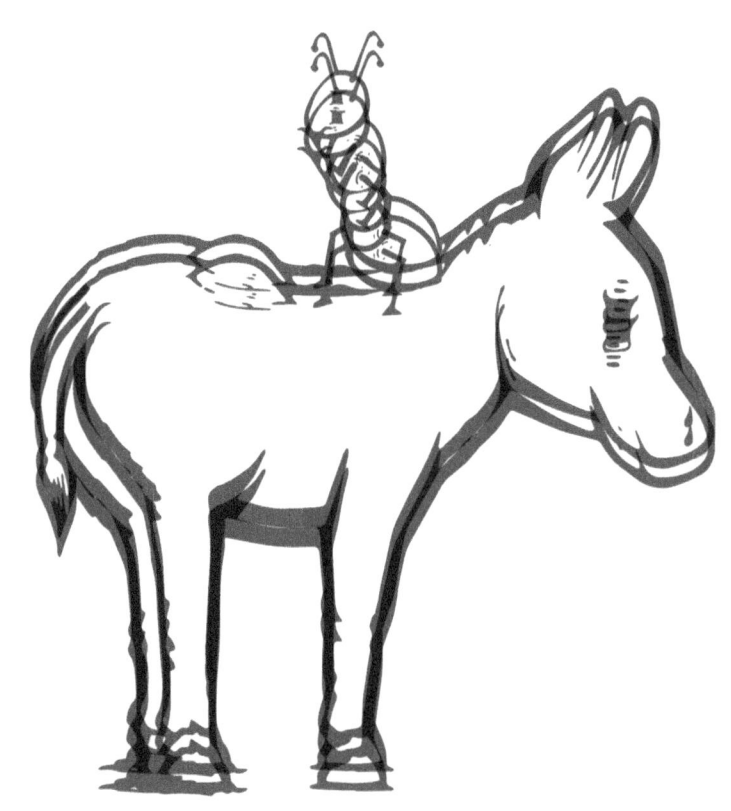

ACE HAD TO GET HELP FIGURING OUT WHAT THE HECK THIS IS.

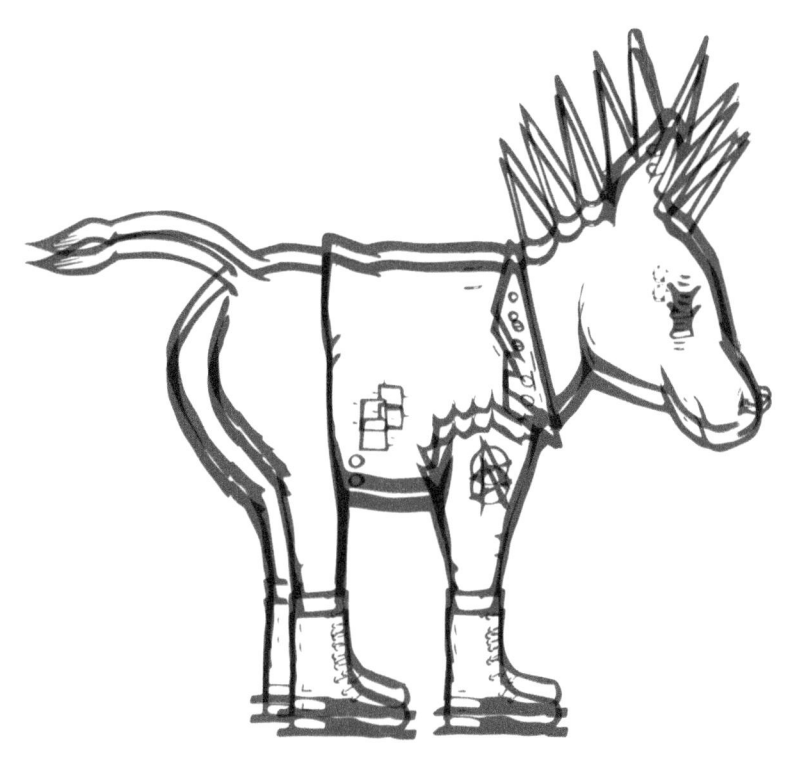

THE EDGY SIDE OF ACE:

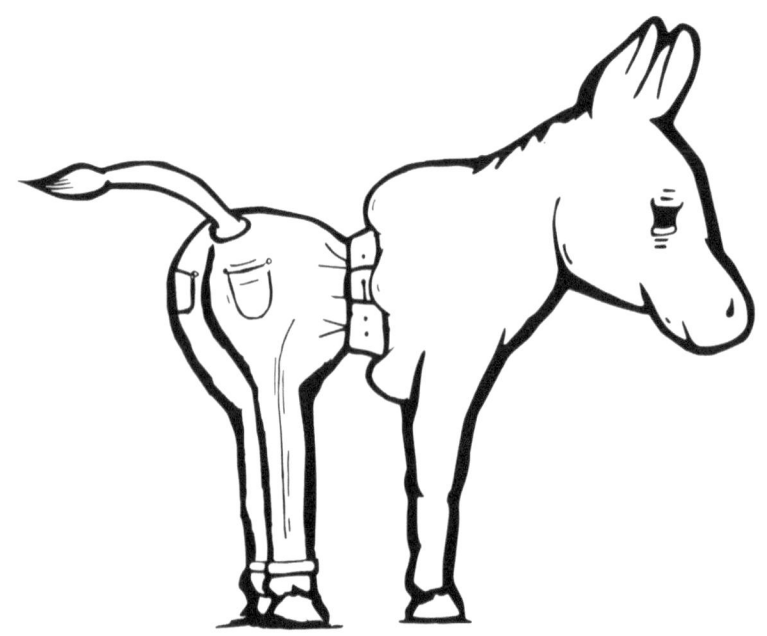

IT TOOK SOME DOING BUT ACE GOT HIMSELF INTO THOSE JEANS.

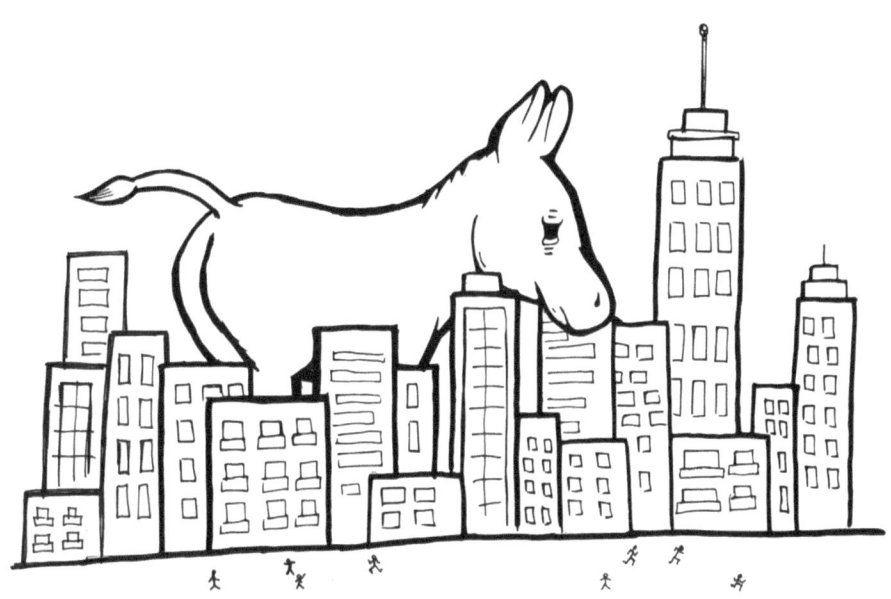

THAT'S ONE HUGE ACE.

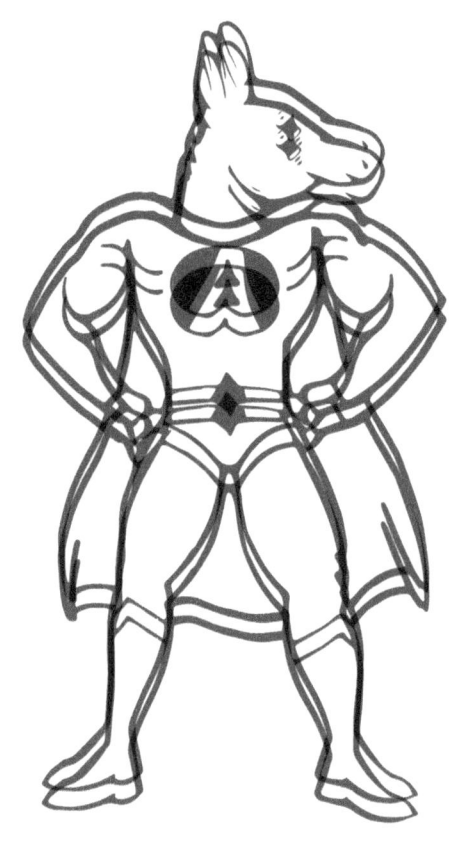

THERE WILL BE A TIME IN YOUR LIFE WHEN YOU WILL BE ASKED WHAT TYPE OF MAN ARE YOU?

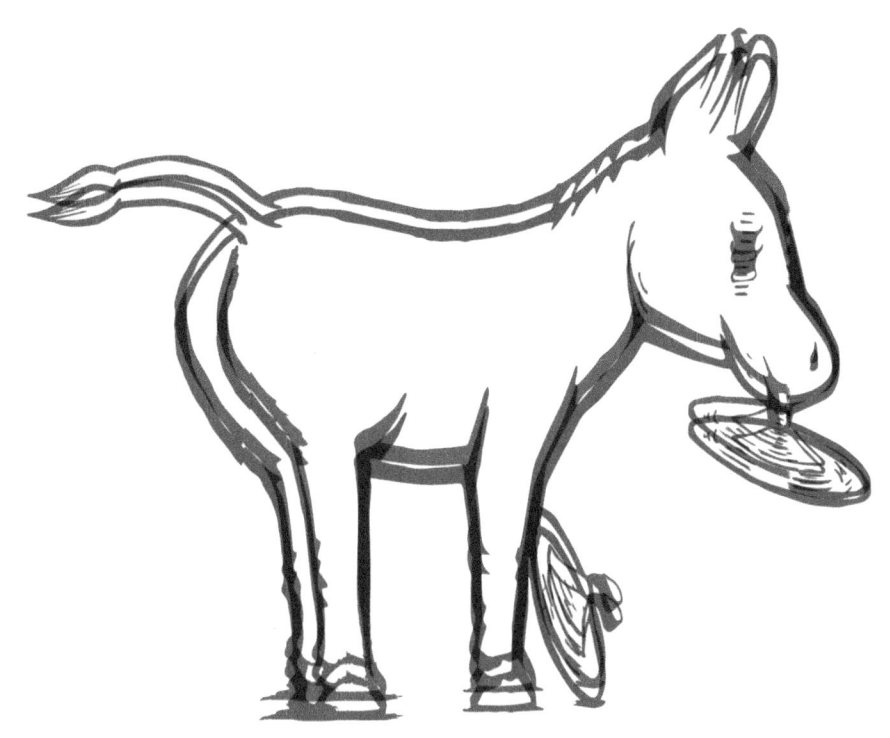

ACE IS EMBRACING HIS 1ST AMENDMENT RIGHTS:

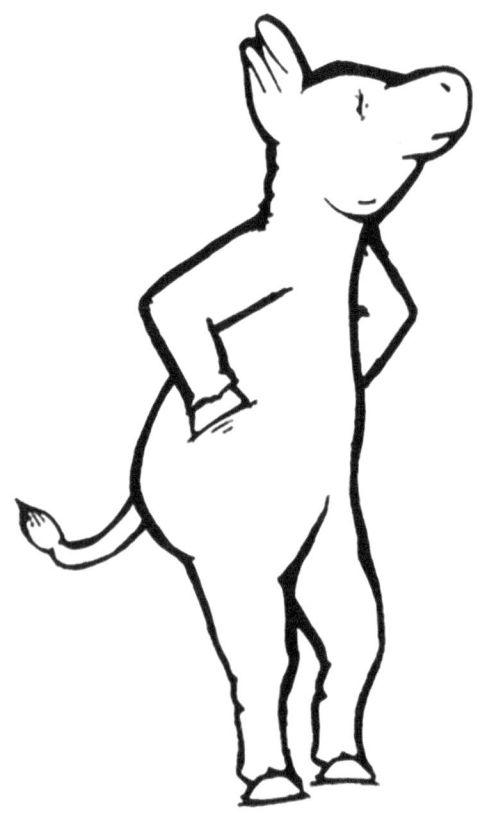

WE ARE GOING TO HAVE TO START CALLING ACE JASON BORNE WITH ALL THIS ATTITUDE.

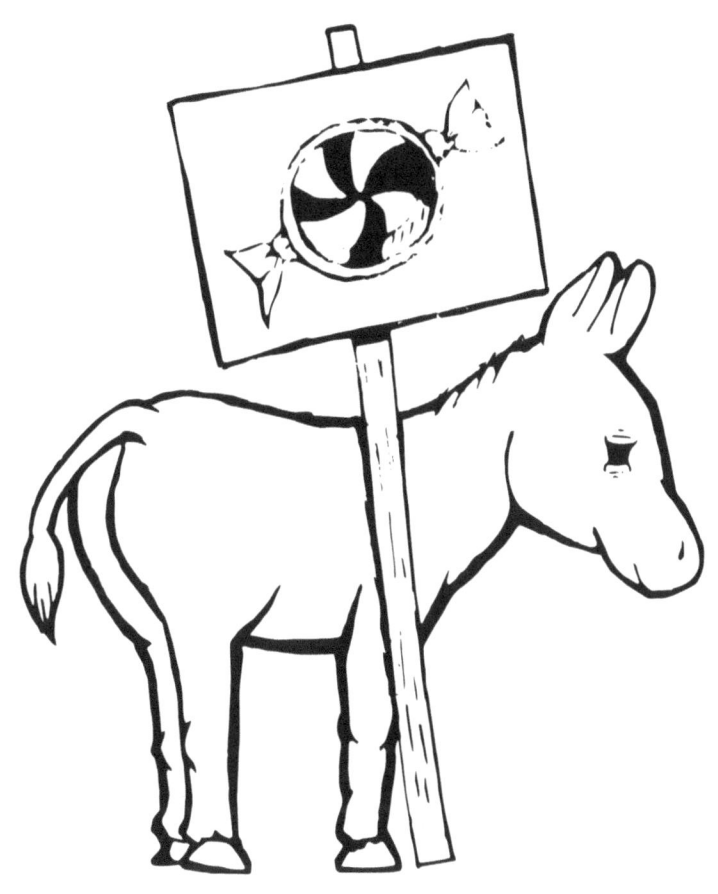

ACE'S TASK FOR TODAY IS TO SHOW HIS SUPPORT FOR MINTS.

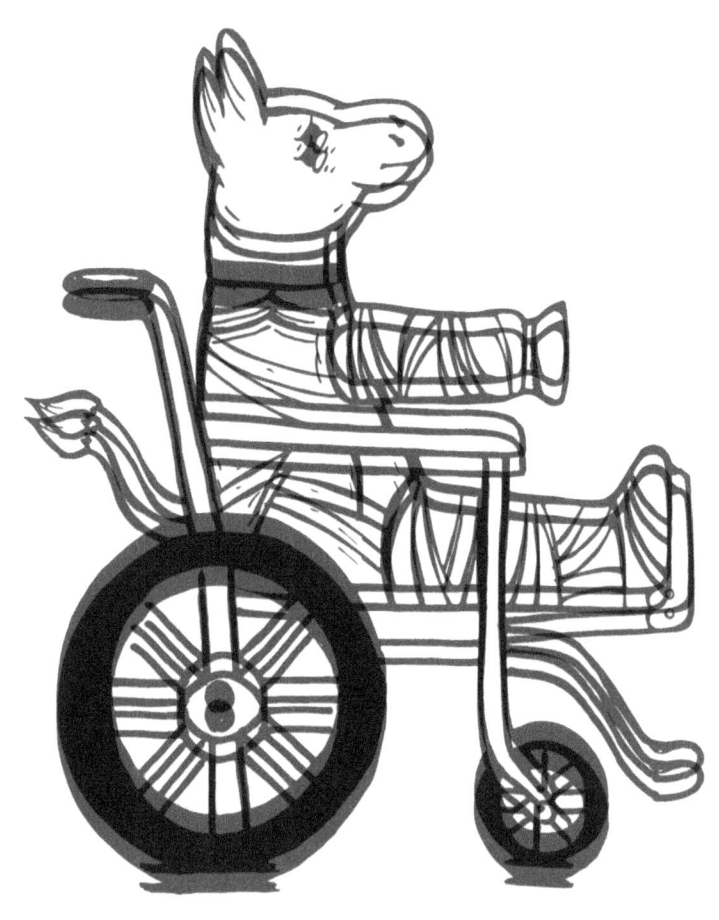

THIS MIGHT COST ACE AN ARM AND A LEG.

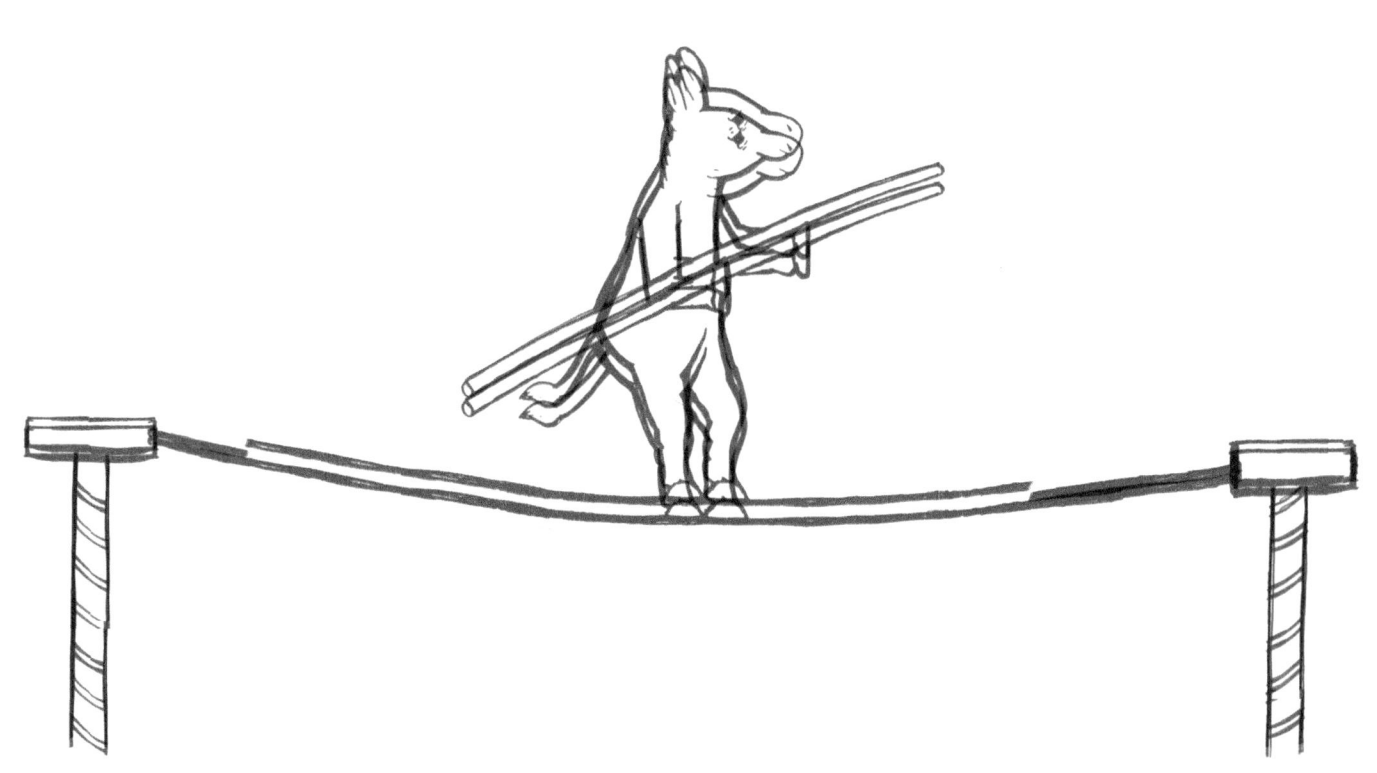

ACE IS TAKING A BIG RISK WTIH THIS STUNT:

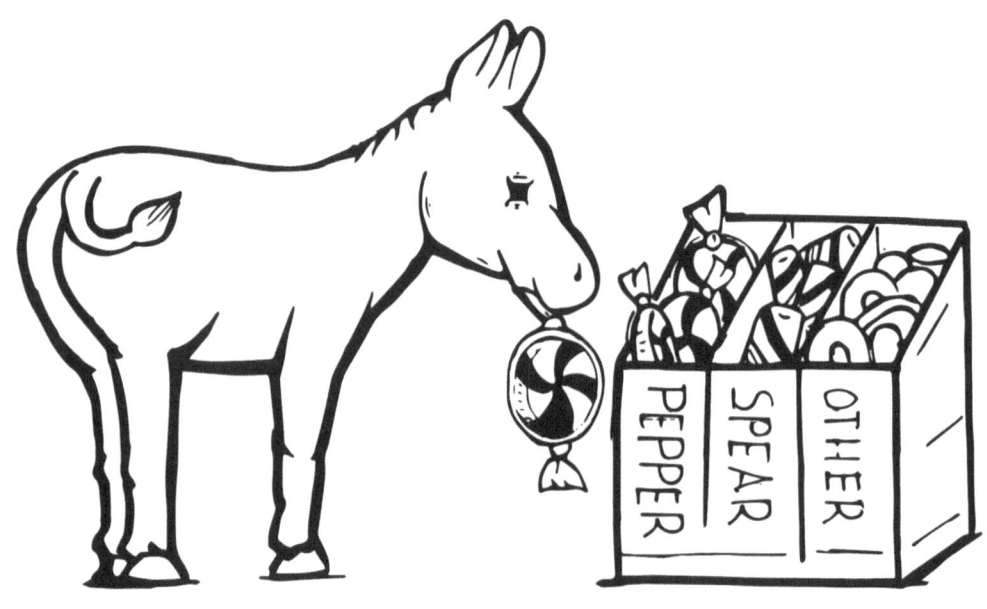

ACE IS ORGANIZING HIS MINTS.

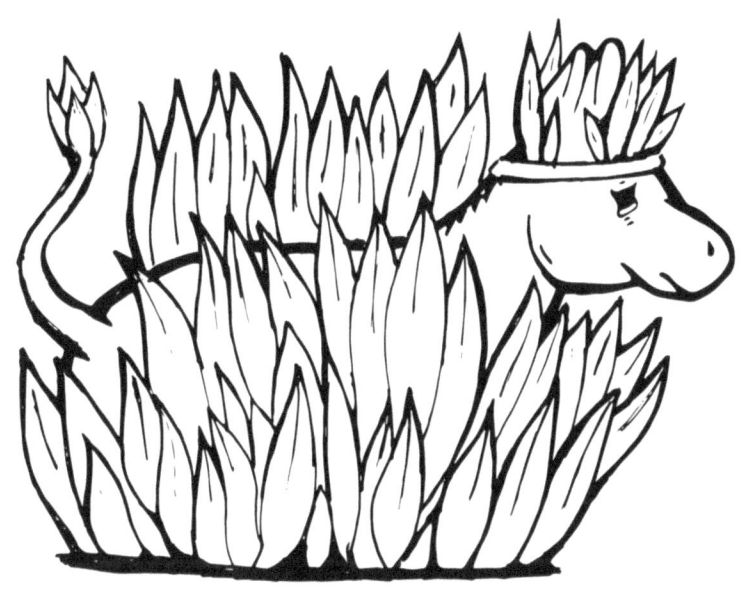

ACE TOOK BEING THREATENED A LITTLE TOO LITERALLY.

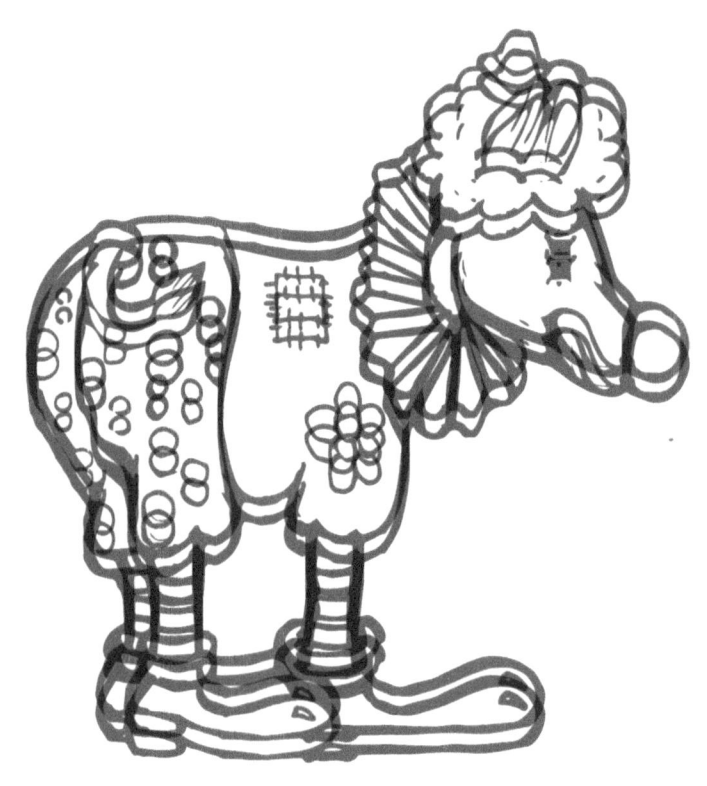

ACE MAKING A FOOL OF HIMSELF:

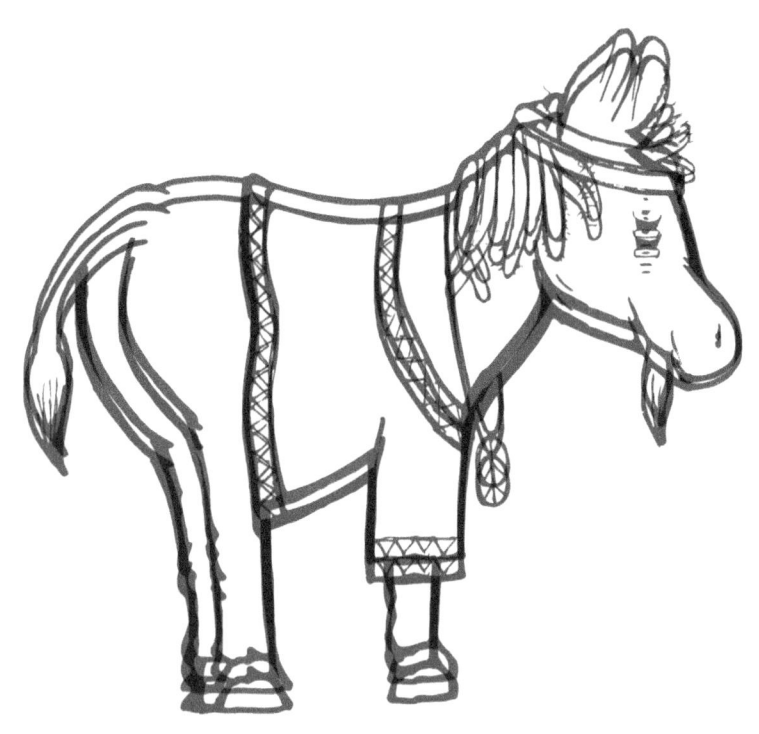

ACE HAD THE NICKNAME OF ED BACK IN THIS PSYCHEDELIC DAYS.

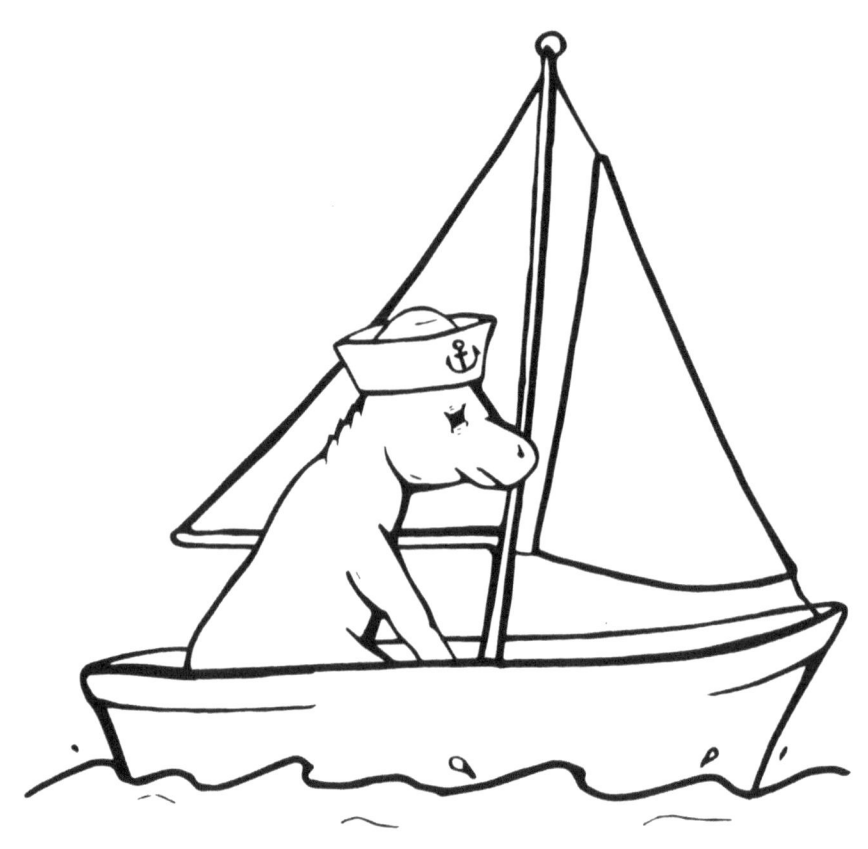

ACE IS ATTACKING THESE WATERS ON HIS SAIL BOAT.

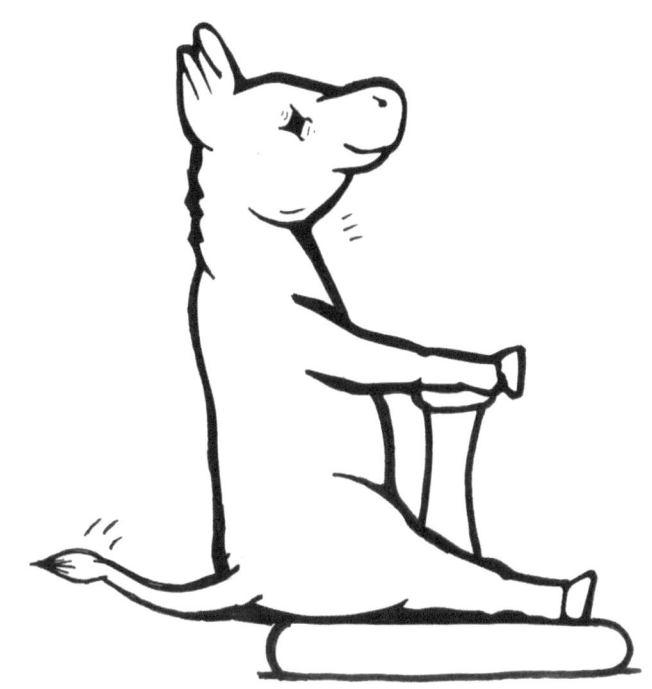

TOWN IN COLORADO, TYPE OF TREE, OR WHATEVER ACE IS DOING.

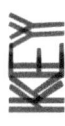 **KEY**

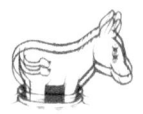	ASSHOLE	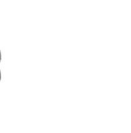	BADASS
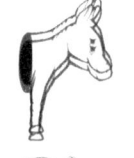	JACKASS	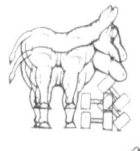	KANSAS
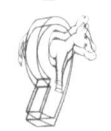	HALF-ASS	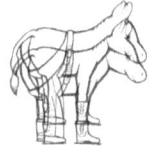	ASTEROID
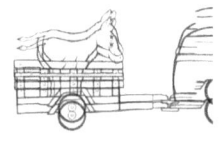	ASININE	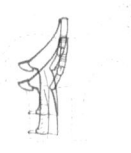	CHAPS MY ASS
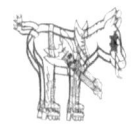	HAULING ASS	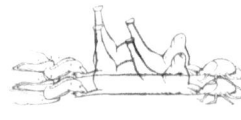	CHAPLESS ASS
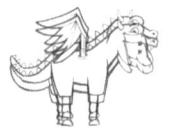	KISS ASS	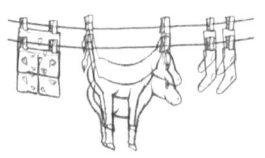	ELASTIC
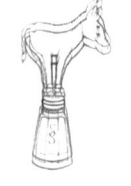	DRAGGIN ASS	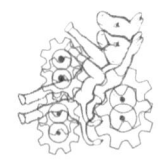	HANG ASS OUT TO DRY
	ASSAULT		ASS IN GEAR

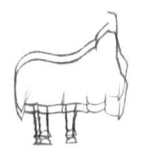 COVER YOUR ASS

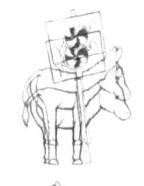 ASSIGNMENT

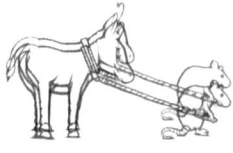 RAT'S ASS

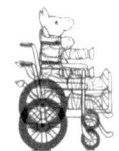 BROKE ASS

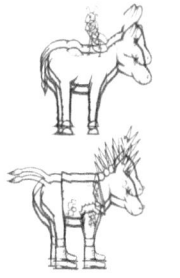 ASSISTANT

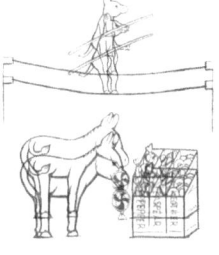 ASS ON THE LINE

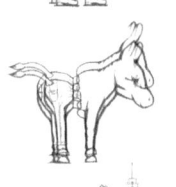 PUNK-ASS

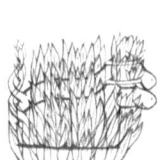 ASSORTMENT

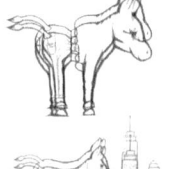 TIGHT-ASS

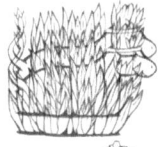 ASS IS GRASS

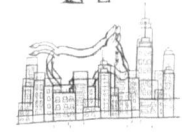 BIG ASS

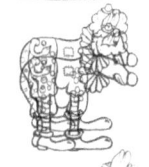 ASS CLOWN

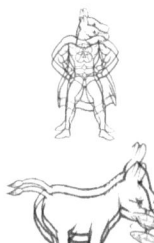 ASS MAN

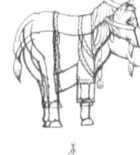 ACID

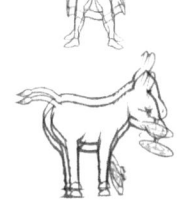 ASSEMBLE

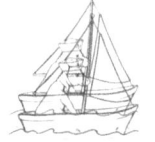 ASSAIL

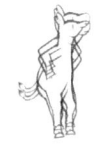 ASSASSIN

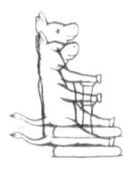 ASPEN

www.ingramcontent.com/pod-product-compliance
Lightning Source LLC
Chambersburg PA
CBHW051934210526
45473CB00006B/2240